PEE SHY
TO
PEE FREE

HOW ONE MAN OVERCAME
AVOIDANT PARURESIS…
AND HOW YOU CAN TOO!

BREAK FREE PRESS

PRINTED IN U.S.A.

BREAK FREE PR E S S

95 GOULD ROAD, #14 LISBON FALLS, MAINE 04252

207-353-5454

PUBLISHERS CATALOGUING IN PUBLICATION DATA
Ledoux, Denis
Pee Shy To Pee Free/A Proven Guide to Overcoming Bashful Bladder
1. Self-improvment.-2. Social Phobias.
I.Title
ISBN-13: 978-1448612550
ISBN-10: 1448612551

ACKNOWLEDGEMENTS

I am grateful to Ross Shaler for the insightful edits and helpful contributions he made throughout the process of writing, editing, and designing Pee Shy to Pee Free. His thoughtful and energetic participation helped the text to become the informative and useful book you now hold. Thank you, Ross.

Table of Contents

Preface: Why Bother?

Driving down the interstate with my friend Jim, I felt that unwelcome sensation of having to urinate but, because I was fearful he would need to go, too, I didn't ask Jim to stop. I didn't want to go into the men's room with him at my heels and stand completely blocked next to him, unable to urinate in the presence of another man.

So, I kept my silence and endured my discomfort.

Finally, (after what clearly seemed an eternity), Jim said, "Let's pull over at the next restaurant. I need to make a pit stop."

At the highway restaurant, I told Jim I didn't need to go, and he entered the restroom by himself. I sat at a restaurant table waiting for him to come back. When he did, we ordered, and I sat through the meal with an uncomfortable bladder that felt like it would burst any minute.

Why am I putting up with this?

-A paruretic

"Don't you want something to drink?" he asked.

"I don't think so," I answer, thinking of how many miles we still have to go. I didn't even touch the water the waitress had placed in front of me.

When we got up to leave, I said in my most innocent voice, "I guess I should go to the men's room after all. Why don't I meet you at the car."

I sauntered into the men's room by myself. If I encountered someone else there, I could always duck into a stall. No one I'd have to be with would know. I wouldn't have to be embarrassed by failure, as I drove down the highway with Jim.

These sorts of uncomfortable situations and likely coping strategies are very familiar to a person who is "pee shy." (We are also said to have "bashful bladder." The technical name is "avoidant paruresis.")

Of course, if you are reading this, you, too, are familiar with coping. Without evasive strategies around urinating, how would you get through your days?

Every once in a while, you have perhaps tried to force yourself to overcome your inhibition, but it has not worked. You have only been repeatedly embarrassed and shamed. In fact, by now, you have probably given up. Better to hone your coping skills, you conclude, than to fail and lose face once again!

Why bother trying to get over paruresis when you know there's no hope?

I am here to tell you there is hope. I am proof that change is possible.

Introduction

Beginning... even when it seems impossible to begin

Some changes seem so difficult. The task of beginning seems not so much hard as impossible. You live with the hope of change but you don't believe it will happen for you. Some part of you has given up.

"For someone else but not for me!"

Perhaps you stare paruresis in the face. It feels like a mortal combat. You want paruresis out of your life, but your inhibition is so strongly entrenched that it is you and not paruresis that blinks. And yet...

Some part of you continues to hope for change.

This is a book about winning the struggle that you have not been winning, about making possible a new reality in your life.

It is not because things are difficult that we do not dare, it is because we do not dare that things are difficult.

—Seneca

This book is about changing behavior. It's about doing something hard. It's about taking a "hero's journey."

Change is not impossible, but it must start with a decision. It requires that you decide—decide to focus on your goal—and that you commit to that goal again and again until you attain it!

Change cannot be achieved by "trying" but by doing the work until change happens. In the end, it must be you and not your past that decides what your behavior will be. (Thoughts and emotions will change, too.)

The choice is yours.

Where you're at is probably not comfortable, but it's your start point.

Congratulations, You've bought this book!

You've taken a first step towards your goal of overcoming your inhibition about urinating in front of other men. You decided to do something about it when you decided to read this book. You could have chosen to moan and groan. To feel sorry for yourself. To give up and say, "I just can't do it." Instead, you decided to change the way things are in favor of the way they will be.

If you apply the steps I am outlining here, you will succeed. They are not hard to follow and yet they are some of the hardest things you will have done in a long time. Afterwards, as you look back from a position of freedom around urination, you will marvel at how you were once afraid of a situation which you now enter into without giving it much thought—unless it be one of relief.

Perhaps there are other ways to overcome "bashful bladder" but the techniques I will propose to you in this book are workable ones that will bring you success. Over the next months to several years (the rate depends on your motivation, level of initial inhibition as well as other factors), you will learn to control your toilet inhibition and perhaps even eventually to eliminate avoidant paruresis entirely.

Perhaps it doesn't seem possible that, one day, you will be free of inhibition. You've been shackled for a long time, and no matter how much you've tried to force yourself when you were blocked, you could not make yourself urinate in public.

But believe me, if you want this inhibition to be over, you can succeed at overcoming it.

It's up to you...

I've been there.

My own bashful bladder has always been inconvenient for me (how's that for an understatement!) and frequently uncomfortable. I might be at a theater and forgo urinating at the intermission because I didn't want the embarrassment that was sure to be with me if I were to go in a public restroom—especially if I were attending with men friends who might be going into the restroom, too, or I had seen men I knew in the audience. As I'm sure you've done, I would sit through the second part of the program, growing increasingly bloated and impatient to have the program end so that I could go home to urinate in private. What dreadful evenings! I could not at all enjoy the productions.

It didn't seem possible to me then that this state of affairs could ever change. It had gone on for so long that my inhibition in public seemed a part of me that would never be different—anymore than my nose or my hair. But...

At one point, I decided I did not want to have this "bashful bladder" in my life anymore. I was determined to do something about it. I wasn't sure what, but I would come up with something. What followed were two years of hopeful but largely unsuccessful attempts at change. And then I came upon the method I am about to outline in this book. Within a year, I went from near total inhibition around public urination to being able to walk into a men's room and stand next to another man and urinate. When I was finally able to urinate next to another man with some regularity, I felt elated, buoyant. I kept saying ecstatically to myself, "I can't believe I'm doing this!"

What's more, incredible as it may seem (because I am still occasionally and unpredictably challenged by this), a few months later, I stood at a urinal trough while another man was present and I was able to urinate using the principles and practices I will outline in this book

What to other men might seem like an insignificant experience was to me a conquest of Everest! I had thought that the freedom I lived in those moments would never be possible in my life.

But it was possible for me to change my behavior and it is possible for you to change yours, too—if that's what you want, if you are willing to do the work to let go of your inhibition and acquire new behavior.

In the scope of the problems you could have in your life, a bashful bladder is very inconveniencing, but it is a minor hassle. If you can keep that in perspective, it may help you to cope with paruresis. This is not to say, however, that bashful bladder is not very awkward. It certainly is and you don't have to put up with it much longer. Change is possible, and you are, at this moment, in the beginning of the process of implementing freedom—your freedom!

How to read this book

Read this book in the order in which it is presented. The first part must be read first since it presents the psychological underpinning of the whole program. The second part is different: there you can jump around as one section or other intrigues you. After you have jumped around and made your way through the book, be sure to read the text at least once in the order I presented the material. That's the way it worked best for me and, if you were right here with me, that's how I'd advise you to read the book: in the order I've made use of it myself.

What you'll need

On the emotional and psychological side, there are many attitudes which will serve you in good stead. You need to bring them to this work. They are optimism and doggedness and a willingness to let go of your fear. And, you must trust my story to guide you.

On the more tangible side, you'll need a journal or notebook in which to review your paruretic past, record and reflect on your current efforts, and write your goals for the future. By journaling your responses to the exercises that are present every few pages, you will become more aware of underlying issues and of what works for you.

You can perhaps succeed without doing the writing exercises, but I think the writing itself will speed up your work. Writing will make you more aware about how you feel and think.

But, you might insist that you already know how you feel and what you think. My observation as a writer and a workshop leader is that you probably don't—at least not as much as you will after you read this book and do its work.

There is always a range of reactions to this request that the reader write in a journal. Some readers will take to it readily and appreciate it for the marvelous tool it is. Others will readily consider writing in the journal as "bullshit," intellectual trickery. If this is you, let me suggest the following:

✓ you do not need to write in full sentences to access your feelings, but later on as you reread your entries, notes in detailed phrases or full sentences will likely be more clear as you review what you wrote.

✓ you can draw and doodle and make charts and paste in pictures from magazines or the Internet, but how about putting in a few words so that later the meaning of these graphics will be clearer?

✓ read what I wrote on witnessing yourself (see page 61) and use the knowledge of the "observant self" to help you focus on the importance of journaling.

If you are doubtful about journal writing being important for effective change (yours), dare risk on paruresis therapy and commit to writing for the duration of your therapy as you do the work of this book. What do you have to lose? Have your past attempts to exorcise paruresis been so effective that you can afford not to try something new?

Good luck

What you are about to do will take you into a new phase of your life. The principles and practices that I will outline for you will not only free you of your bashful bladder but they will also affect other areas of your life in ways that you are not able to anticipate now. Once mastered, these principles and practices can be applied to many other facets of your life so that change elsewhere may not only be a by-product but a goal in itself.

But, for now, you are focused on resolving a particular issue, and this book will help you do that. Anything else will come later.

I am sure of this, and you can be assured of it, too: you will succeed if you apply the principles and practices outlined in these pages.

Good luck.

Chapter 1: Background

The only statement I can make with certainty about your bashful bladder is that it is shame-based. I don't know the specific source of this shame and you probably don't either but shame's crip- pling nature is much the same for all of us—for me and for you.

The child is father of the man.
—Wordsworth

At some point, around the issue of urination, someone or something got to you. Most likely, you were made to feel inadequate or soiled, or wrong, or defective. Whatever...

How did paruresis enter your life? What are its origins?

✓ **Perhaps paruresis started as early as your toilet training.** Perhaps your parents were demeaning about your ability to be continent. Perhaps you were a bed wetter, and your parents shamed you most awfully in the mornings when your sheets were wet—or perhaps it was your siblings. Or, perhaps again, it was your fear of others knowing about your bed wet- ting—at school, at cub scouts—and your belief that they would make fun of you that shut you down.

✓ **Perhaps older boys at school taunted you in the toilets.**

"What's the matter!? Your weewee doesn't pee right, little boy?" they jeered.

"Your pecker too little to hold, kid?"

Perhaps you had no problems with paruresis just then but, in time, the hazing began to get to you. One day, you began to avoid the toilet room when other boys were there. Then, you began to avoid the boy's room even when it was empty. Eventually, you needed to have more and more privacy even at home.

✓ **Perhaps the men in your family were condescending.** When you urinated with them outdoors, they made "cute" comments about your "little thing." You began avoiding having your "little thing" out in the open.

✓ **Perhaps modesty was paramount in your family.** Urination was relegated to the most secret of secrets. Anything having to do with the body was to be hidden in shame. How could you possibly be so immodest as to expose your penis in front of others?

✓ **Perhaps your mother (or other women in your family) did not like men.** She made comments about how dirty men were when they urinated. She made disparaging remarks about penises and abusive comments about men's bodies (and emotions) in general. How could you possible be comfortable with urination—which at that time was the only use for your penis you knew of?

✓ **Perhaps you were sexually abused.** Every time you stuck your dick out, it felt like you were about to be assaulted once again. A men's room, open to the male public, filled with strangers, was the last place you wanted to risk anything. When you had to go in, you were extremely guarded. It began to be difficult to urinate there.

✓ **Perhaps it began in conujunction with**

your sexual awakening. In the fifth and sixth grades, you noticed that other boys had larger penises and some were sporting pubic hair. Nothing like that was happening to you. You began to be ashamed of your anatomy and not wanting to be seen sticking your penis out. Perhaps, you concluded, you were not a real boy in some way.

Story from the field

For a long time, when I would walk into men's rooms, I would look around. I was looking for it to be empty. If it was, I would assure myself I was safe. If there was someone else there, I would leave.

One day, I entered a men's room thinking it was empty, but it wasn't.

As soon as I saw the other man, an unexpected presence, I was overcome with incredible TERROR. I felt like I was loosing my contact with the present and the place. For a moment, it was as if I were a little boy again and I was about to be abused at the hands of this man.

Fortunately, he left soon and I was able to calm myself down, to assure myself that I was a grown man capable of taking care of myself.

✓ **Perhaps you had some ambivalence about your sexuality.** Did you like boys or did you like girls? Every time you went into the boys' room you began to have uncomfortable feelings. Toilets were increasingly associated with feelings you didn't want to have. Even today, perhaps you have not owned your attraction towards men.

✓ **Perhaps in college you were out of your element and not successful and felt "less than."** Other young men seemed to be having better grades and were scoring with the girls and you began to feel that you were deficient. Your sense of yourself as a person and as a man began to be associated with urination and your difficulties with it grew.

✓ **Perhaps it's none of these or perhaps it's many of these.** Every case is unique, but every case is perhaps connected to shame.

Knowing the probable cause of your paruresis will not "cure" the problem, but it will help you to diffuse it. (See cognitive therapy, Page 65.)

Whatever the cause, you can overcome paruresis. It is something that has happened to you, something that is in your life, but it is not something that you are.

Letting paruresis remain in your life or going beyond it is now a matter of choice—yours.

Exercise

In your journal, write about what you consider to be the origins of your paruresis. Include:
  ✓ your best guess about its roots,
  ✓ your early memories of being pee shy,
  ✓ your recollection of an embarrassing time with urination,
  ✓ what seems to help the most now to get you to urinate more easily,
  ✓ a recent incident—how is it different and the same as the incident in your early memories?

The grip of paruresis

Regardless of its origins, paruresis has you in its grip!

What is certain is that you reacted to something by withdrawing from urinating anywhere anyone could observe you and perhaps judge you. In some (unconscious) part of yourself, you said, "I'm getting negative energy around urinating in front of others, and I'm going to protect myself by urinating only in private. That is the behavior that I am going to adopt."

Keep this in mind: while you may be interested in finding the origins of your bashful bladder, it is not necessary to know how paruresis began to lessen its grip and effect change. What is necessary is action, a conscious change of behavior. Your action will be helped by your awareness of the feelings that surround your public urination.

How does shame-based behavior work?

Shamed-based behavior thrives on secrecy, and bashful-bladder is a shameful behavior.

Look at how your paruresis survives and thrives. Don't you hide your bashful bladder syndrome from everyone—or nearly everyone—you know? Don't you go to great lengths to keep it a secret? Sometimes, don't you even hide it from yourself? Haven't you foregone a trip to the restroom because "I really don't need to go" or "I can wait."

Bashful bladder shows its shameful self anytime you are inhibited from urinating in a situation in which it would be appropriate to urinate and which would not intimidate other men. Bashful bladder can occur in a public men's room or with friends alongside a hiking trail or on a sailboat where other men urinate over the side but you wait more and more painfully until you get back to shore—and to the privacy you need to urinate in secrecy.

Is paruresis a wide-spread problem? (Or, is it only me who is sneaking around?)

Because you don't speak about paruresis, you think you are the only one with this phobia.

But are you the only person with avoidant paruresis? No, I read a newspaper article that stated one in twelve men have some significant difficulty with public urination—whether occasionally or habitually. That's a lot of men and a lot of discomfort.

Story from the Field

When I told Matthew about my paruresis, he had a glint of recognition and laughed. I knew he wasn't laughing at me and I waited for his comment.

"There was a one-user men's room and I was the only one waiting in line. The man who had been inside stepped out, and I proceeded to enter when another man came rushing towards the door and entered with me.

"I've got to go bad," he said. "Do you have a problem if I come in with you? I just can't wait."

There we were both inside, and I had already begun to unzip. Yeah, I minded—I was nervous. "What if I couldn't go?" I thought. Perhaps I should just step out and leave the guy have the room? But, I said, "Sure, no bother."

We stood at our respective sides of the toilet. He started right away, and it took me a moment longer but I started, too. He was just talking as if we were just standing anywhere, doing just anything.

It was like being a kid—pissing together into the bowl.

"For a moment, though, I felt a twinge of what must be what you call *paruresis*."

Exercise

Write about the feeling/thought you have
  ✓ when you first become aware that you need to go pee. Go into detail. Are these feelings you welcome or do they weigh you down?
  ✓ when you enter a men's room. What do you notice, how do you respond?
  ✓ when you notice other men there, what is your reaction?
  ✓ what is your current coping strategy? Describe in detail how you feel about it?

Perhaps a majority of men are faced with some degree of self-awareness around urinating in front of others. The difference between them and you however is that their self-awareness is not a blocker.

Our self-awareness, unlike Matthew's, is crippling and blocks us from continuing. (Reading the above story, what was your reaction? Horror? Envy? Almost certainly not: "Oh, sure, I'd have done just like Matthew.")

You are not alone.

One in twelve is a high percentage. If you haven't noticed paruretic men already when you're in a public restroom (and incredibly some men with bashful bladder have not), you'll notice more and more how some guys enter toilet stalls to urinate or hesitate on walking into a restroom and, finding you (and possibly others) there, wash their hands. Or, perhaps they stand a long time at a urinal without any apparent action and, after a quick flush, hurry out.

While I do not take any comfort in the difficulties these men face, after I became aware of them, it was reassuring to realize that I was not the only one—some sort of freak.

Story from the Field

Over the weekend, I walked into a men's room to find a row of three urinals. A man was at #1, and I was going for #3 when I decided, "Hell, I'll do #2 and stand next to the guy." Up the ante—why not!

At #2, I had no trouble urinating. While doing so, I realized that that fellow next to me was having trouble. Yikes! I felt real bad. "I got to get out," I thought. "Leave him privacy to piss."

In the past, I had always rushed out. That day, I realized I could not take care of the man. My commitment had to be to my own growth. All I could do was take care of myself, do what I had to do—urinate, wash my hands, straighten my clothes, etc.

When I left the room, he was still there. One thing I can say is I know how he felt struggling to urinate while someone else was in the room!

Excercise

In restrooms, have you noticed men who seemed to have difficulty urinating? If so, write about the experience. Include:
✓ How did they behaved?
✓ What was their body posture?
✓ How did you feel noticing them?
✓ Did noticing inhibit you more or free you in some way?
Now write about noticing men who have no difficulty. Include the same points as above.

Chapter 2: Behavior Modification

Behaviors are not innate. You were not born with any of the behaviors—positive or negative—that now characterize your life. All behaviors are learned—and therefore can be unlearned.

Since toilet habits are behaviors and therefore learned, they can be unlearned and replaced with other behaviors *of your choosing.* If you are willing to do the work, you can rid yourself of shamed-based behaviors and fill your days with behaviors that are more life-supportive.

It will take time, effort, and concentration, but these can be your allies rather than your foes as you reach for success.

Change is possible, and it is up to you.

Behaviors and emotions

There are two areas to focus on as you unlearn an inappropriate behavior and learn an appropriate one:

✓ behavior modification and its close, but secondary, companion,

✓ emotional/psychological transformation.

These two foci are separate—and closely linked. Inhibition around public urination is a behavior problem, best modified by gradual behavior change. Sure, emotional/psychological work will speed up the process, but it is not likely to be sufficient by itself. The two together are your strongest bet.

In our work in this book, you will notice that, although the writing sometimes leads me to create a distinction between behavioral and psychological work and I have established separate sections to deal with each, I often write about both together in the same section as if they were intermixed. That's because they are, and I couldn't do otherwise than write about them together.

Even so, it is behavior modification—change in what you do—which must always receive your priority attention. Change your behavior and you will change your feeling.

Your nervous system

Your body via its nervous system has learned to be uptight and tense when urinating in public. You think about a men's room, and your pelvis tightens. You go into a men's room, and it's total down time.

This may now seem to you like your natural response. ("I've always been this way. It's just me!"), but it is not a natural response at all. It is a response you have learned in order to cope with something that belongs to your past rather than to your present. (Review "Possible Origins...," page 15, also see 62)

The bad news is that your paruresis is now embedded in your unconscious nervous system, but here is the good news: like all learned responses, it can be replaced by another response which you can equally learn and embed in your nervous system. The choice is really yours.

Your nervous system is made of two parts: the **conscious** and the **unconscious**. The **conscious system** controls all those aspects of your physical and emotional being that you can affect: moving your big toe, acting as if you are grateful, etc. When you stand at a urinal and try to force the urine out through an act of will, you are calling on the conscious nervous system. As you know from your experience of trying to force yourself to pee, the conscious nervous system cannot overrule the unconscious where paruresis has taken hold of your behavior. You can force yourself as much as you want, but your experience tells you it's almost guaranteed that your urine will not flow. Most likely, only when the room is emptied of other men will you be able at last to urinate.

To overcome paruresis, you need a strategy that goes beyond the conscious nervous system. Only then will you be able to cope with your inhibition whose roots are in the unconscious.

The **unconscious system** has two parts also— the **sympathetic** and the **parasympathetic**. The first is an expanding, accelerating system while the second is a contracting, slowing-down one.

The **sympathetic system** is the flight or fight program that you use whenever you feel under attack. It makes your heart beat more quickly, your blood pulse, your skin flush. Does this sort of physical reaction seem familiar? Does this description remind you of the flush you get when you stand at a urinal, knowing there's no way you'll ever urinate no matter how bad you have to go and how hard you try?

The parasympathetic system, however, has the opposite effect. It calms you down. Sleep is a strong example of the parasympathetic system—and so is meditation.

The task ahead of you is to learn to minimize the effects of the sympathetic "fight or flight" system and maximize the parasympathetic system.

Meditation is crucial in beating avoidant paruresis.

You can train yourself to be in the parasympathetic system more frequently and for longer periods of time by meditating. Meditators tend to be more relaxed and therefore more likely to remain calm during crises. (Going into men's rooms to urinate is a "fight or flight" crisis for paruretics!)

Once you learn to relax your body through meditation, you will be both generally more relaxed in your life and you will be able to apply the relaxation consciously (to various degrees) whenever you are in a situation that tenses you up. So when you must urinate in public and you begin to get nervous, you can practice deep breathing and detachment. This will counteract the flight or fight syndrome which tightens your urinary tract muscles. Being able to relax and detach will serve you well in overcoming paruresis.

Briefly, mindfulness meditation consists of observing your breath. Sit at a comfortable chair. Unloosen your collar button and your belt. (You need to be able to breathe freely.) Close your eyes and breathe slowly but comfortably through your nose. Experience your breath coming in and going out. From your nose to your lungs. Feel yourself breathe deeply and let your diaphragm expand. Pause. Then slowly breathe out. It's really not complicated. Every time you complete a breath cycle (in and out) say the number of that breathe (one, two, etc.).

On the "in" breath, imagine the air entering through your head and descending through your body and exiting via your perineum (the base of your torso). On the "out" breath, imagine the air entering through the perineum and rising through your body to exit via the top of the skull. This alternation establishes a comfortable breath cycle. Every odd breath is from top to bottom, and every even breath is from bottom to top. In a short while, your breathing will become rhythmical.

I would suggest either three sessions of 150 breaths or two sessions of 200 per day. Whichever you choose, space it over the day—morning and evening and possibly in the middle of the day.

There are many books on meditation available. They can do a better job of instructing you than I can. If you have never meditated, try reading several of these books cover to cover and doing the exercises they suggest. Meditation is, of course, not something you do once. You need to meditate every day. Admittedly, meditation is boring, but so is paruresis! (Which would you rather commit yourself to?)

If you meditate regularly, you will find yourself looking forward to the quiet time it affords you. And you will be amazed at how you can draw on its quiet strength as you do the warrior work of overcoming your paruresis.

Exercise
✓ Find a comfortable spot where you can sit quietly and undisturbed. ✓ Meditate for five minutes. The next time you meditate, do so for ten minutes and, the time after that, for fifteen minutes. ✓ In your journal, write about your experience of meditating. How did you feel after meditating?

Behavior modification vs. understanding

Paruresis is a problem of the unconscious. Inhibition developed in response to conditioning. You slipped into paruretic behavior as a means of avoiding some other pain—usually psychological and emotional.

"If behavior got you into this mess, behavior can also get you out of it."

That cause, that stimulus, is most likely not there in your environment any more. For instance, the bullying boys have long since grown up and are probably civilized guys. They may even have turned into decent men. But, that doesn't make a difference, because the unconscious does not live in our time. Today or thirty years ago are the same time. Those boys are still very much bullies for the uncontious.

Paruresis is somehow embedded in our nervous system. Our task is to embed another behavior there now. And as paruresis probably developed over a period of time (in a process of graduated descent into inhibition) so too can you rise out of the paruretic mire through graduated behavior change over time.

28

If you have ever lifted weights, you now that, at the beginning of your gym experience, certain weights were well beyond your ability to move. Later, after having committed to lifting regularly and attentively, you were able to lift the very weight that had once seemed impossible.

What made the difference was a change in your behavior. You took on serious lifting behavior. It was repeated lifting and not understanding the philosophy of lifting that made the difference. No amount of knowledge of the musculature of your body would have by itself effected a difference in your ability to lift.

This is not to say that knowledge of musculature cannot be extremely helpful. For instance, if you want to improve your bench press, you need to improve your triceps as your triceps are essential in lifting a weight off your chest. This bit of knowledge will lead you to do triceps' specific strength exercises. These in turn will jack your bench press faster than doing bench presses in isolation.

The same is true with overcoming paruresis. Knowledge of your past difficulties and of effective adaptations will be useful to you in setting up the appropriate behavior modification exercises. Using your knowledge, you will create and practice certain exercises rather than others. This will speed your progress as you will not waste time with behavior modification sequences that are not developmental for you. It will help you with cognitive therapy that will be discussed later. (see page 65) But, any amount of knowledge without graduated exposure work which I go into in the next chapter, however much energy and excitement knowledge might recruit, will simply not be your solution to paruresis. (Just as triceps work without bench pressing will not jumpstart your bench press!)

Chapter 3: Graduated Exposure

As the name says, behavior modification is a technique for changing the way one does things, modifying how one behaves.

In weightlifting, progressive overload is the key. In time, as a result of regularly increasing the weights, the repetitions or the sets, a person can learn to lift weights beyond what he had originally been capable of, even beyond what he might have thought ultimately possible.

The equivalent of progressive overload for behavior modification is graduated exposure. Graduated exposure calls for slowly increasing the difficulty of the conditions under which you attempt to urinate in the presence of others. Step by more challenging step, you will arrive at the freedom you desire.

"Inch by inch, it's a cinch. Yard by yard, it's hard."

In order to assure a gradation of exposure that is appropriate for you, I will help you to create a ranking of situations that are difficult for you to urinate in. The first item on your list is the one in which you are currently comfortable most of the time, in which you almost never have any difficulty urinating. Then place the scenario that is at the next level of difficulty. Some scenarios will be equally difficult. How to choose one over the other? Place one first and then the other—your choice! (Jumping levels is a set up for failure!) In this way, step by step, you will arrive at listing your most desired (and feared!) situations.

Being at ease in each of these settings is your goal.

A Sample Exposure Ranking: The Room Itself

The following shaded boxes were my own exposure ranking of men's room set ups. Yours may have many of the same steps, but then, your ranking may be quite different. It may start with a closed, locked one-user room or with a row of urinals without separators. Whatever step is your baseline of comfort, that will be your first graduated exposure exercise.

I placed my ranking into two groups: the men's room itself which I write about in this section and the people who may be in there with me which I write about in the next section. The divisions are not strict and you may find loopholes in them, but they worked for me. Feel free to copy any step that works for you.

Since I could almost always urinate in a "Single urinal separated by a wall from the rest of the room with someone else in the room" that became my baseline. To be certain that I wasn't deluding myself about my level, I tried it several times. I was successful each time so I was ready to move on to a "Row of urinals with wall separators and at least one empty spot between me and the other man."

Almost Never Any Room Problem
1. Stall even with others in the room who are not paying attention to me. 2. Single urinal blocked off with no one conversing with me. 3. Alone in any restroom.

In Increasing Order of Room Challenge

1. Single urinal separated by a wall from the rest of the room with someone else in the room.
2. Row of urinals with full wall separators and at least one empty spot between me and the other man.
3. Row of urinals with partial separators and at least one empty spot between me and the other man.
4. Alone in the room and at a row of urinals that is without separators and that is fully visible from the entrance with the possibility of someone walking in.
5. Alone at a long row of urinals with men in back of me talking to each other.
6. At a single urinal with a wall but someone speaking to me about banal things (weather, etc.).
7. At a row of urinals with a wall but someone speaking to me about something that requires a response.
8. Arriving at urinals at the same time as someone.
9. At a row of urinals, no walls, someone speaking to me.
10. At a row of urinals, no walls, with space between me and another man. No speaking.
11. At two urinals combo with someone next to me.
12. Someone at urinals on each side of me with no walls or separator in between.
13. At a trough, alone, with someone in the room.
14. At a trough, with someone at the other end.
15. At a trough, with someone on either side of me.
16. At a trough, with someone I know.
17. At a trough, with someone I don't know speaking to me.
18. At a trough, with someone I know speaking to me.

Excercise
✔ Write your list of exposure rankings. ✔ Try your baseline situation at least three or four times to ascertain that you are not fooling yourself about your level. ✔ Once you have been successful 3 or 4 times, move on to item number two on your list.

Another Sample Exposure Ranking: The Men Inside

In doing this work, I soon realized that there was an important factor beyond the layout of the men's room itself. Who was present with me in the restroom and what he or they were doing was also significant. A situation that may have been very do-able with a certain kind of man doing a certain kind of activity was nearly impossible with another sort of man doing the same or another sort of activity.

The following ranking tried to address this.

Almost Never Any People Problem
1. A man alone with me with whom I have spoken about my paruresis and with whom I have practiced at least once. 2. A room with many men and some milling around.

Unlike the physical aspects of a men's room which are stable and can be counted on to remain the same for your next visit, who is in the room is always changing and, most of the time, you can only count on the composition being unpredictably different at your next visit. (An exception might be a workplace restroom where some of the same men go at some of the same times.)

In Increasing Order of People Challenge

1. With someone who is near leaving but still at a urinal.
2. Stall with someone speaking to me.
3. Young masculine man in the room.
4. Young masculine man in the row of urinals.
5. Someone saying as we approach the urinal at about the same time. "You go first!" and then waiting as he does something else.
6. Someone saying as we approach the urinal at about the same time. "You go first!" and then waiting directly in back of me.
7. Someone I know is in the room.

Even given the unpredictability, there is some graduated exposure you can practice. My third item "Young masculine man in the room" and my fourth "Young masculine man in the row of urinals" are clearly workable. I have the option of doing some emotional work around these categories so that the intimidation they elicit can be lessened or eliminated. (Introspection, meditation, affirmations are all clearly helpful. The last two are written about lower down.) In addition, when I am ready, I can also go to restrooms frequented by young men. For instance, I can go to a bar that caters to the young (it's often possible to walk in and out without being a patron), go to a sports venue, or use university rest rooms.

As with your behavior vis-a-vis the rest room itself, your behavior with the occupants of a rest room can be modified to become more positive and functional. You can eventually become more who you want to become.

For example, you can practice sample conversations that are appropriate with strangers in a rest room (the weather, or some such topic). Script it out and practice on your own. Then when the occasion presents itself slip into the conversation.

Some of these situations which are (usually unwittingly) made challenging by the presence of other men can be replicated with the pee buddy exposure I write about in the next chapter. You will find that an excellent way to diffuse the charge of these situations. (After you have read that chapter, com back to review this one.)

Men's Rooms in Your Area

Another important list is that of the public restrooms in your area categorized in order of difficulty. It must include spots that make it possible to practice the first five items (at least) on your graduated exposure list. Identify restrooms that are close enough for you to practice every day—or at least four or five times a week. (In the beginning, frequency seems to be very useful. Closely spaced exposure will incrementally speed up your progress.) The list ought to include fast food restaurants, large stores, and malls. It possible to use restrooms off hotel lobbies. Just be sure you choose venues with enough traffic to balance the effort of getting there with the exposure you can get.

"It takes time and attention to change one's behavior, but it can be done."

Arrange your practice around times when you have to be out and about anyway—that will circumvent the excuse of "I don't have time!" Drink water beforehand and refrain from emptying your bladder in the hour before you leave home.

Story from the Field

Needing to go big time, Guy walked into a restroom to find a man leaning against a stall partition talking to another man at one of two urinals.

Guy really had to go so he walked behind the chatting man to get to the free urinal. He found himself, cheek by jowl, beside the man at the other urinal—a situation which, by itself, would have intimidated him. Behind Guy was an extrovert who was furiously defending a point.

Guy was feeling great pressure. He couldn't imagine the situation being more intimidating.

Soon, the talker brought Guy into the conversation and began to slap him enthusiastically on the back as he was attempting to relieve himself.

Imagine being in mid-stream and being engaged in a jocular conversation with someone slapping you on the back! Because he had to go so bad, he focused on getting his stream going. He ignored the man and did not return the chatter.

Finally, the man left. This permitted Guy to finish. It seems the man at the second urinal didn't know the talker either and it caused him to break urinal etiquette by talking to say, "I thought he'd never leave!"

Men's Rooms at a Distance

Sometimes, you need more than the local restroom can offer you. You may have to drive some to practice in more challenging restroom situations than available locally. (The trough, for instance.)

Again, as you begin to practice at some distance,

identify public rest rooms with a significant traffic of men. Malls and airports, for instance, generally offer large facilities with much coming and going. The value of these high-traffic venues is two fold:

1. if you "block," you can leave the scene without urinating and, within five minutes, return to practice to a whole new cast of bathroom characters (who do not know you blocked five minutes earlier). This will minimize the sense of embarrassment and "weirdness."

2. if you do it right, you can get more practice. In these airport and mall visits, urinate only slightly, only enough to practice starting which is usually the hardest part. If you do not empty your bladder and immediately drink a lot of liquid, you will need to urinate again relatively soon. This will increase your practice time.

Be sure these visits are scheduled around high use times. I once scheduled a visit to our regional airport during a two hour period when there were no "in" or "out" flights. Needless to say, the restrooms were empty for most of the duration, and I left without much practice.

Rehearsing Behaviors

Perhaps you are now comfortable with certain restroom arrangements, but...

✓ what if you walk into a restroom you've never been in and the room is different from what you expected and it is clearly at another level of exposure?

✓ what if you are at one step on the exposure ranking and feel you are not making any progress toward getting to the next?

How can you ever get beyond these stuck places? One way to move on taking the next step is to rehearse it. You can rehearse mentally—not at the rest room—or you can rehearse in the rest room itself. These rehearsals are also called visualization.

Story from the Field

Ted was hiking with his friend Bill. They were looking out over a mountain vista when Bill unzipped his fly and took his penis out and began to urinate. This made Ted so nervous that he had to walk away and leave Bill for the few moments it took Bill to relieve himself.

Later, when at home watching TV, Ted saw a scene in which several men met by happenstance in a rest room and began negotiating a business arrangement. Two of the men had been washing their hands and had obviously finished using the room while the third walked off camera. Although the camera did not show the man urinating, nor could Ted hear any sound, it was obvious what the man was doing as the other two men continued to talk to each other and to him. Ted got very anxious, his heartbeat quickened, and he wanted the scene to be over.

Ted realized he was very uncomfortable not only about his own public urination but about that of other men. It seemed easiest to start his work of dealing with paruresis with increasing his comfort level around others urinating. As he monitored his behavior, he became aware that he rushed through washing his hands and combing his hair in a restroom if other men were urinating. He was nervous about witnessing them do so. He resolved to take his time while in men's rooms and to repeat to himself, "I am comfortable around other men urinating." (See affirmations, page 44.) He even took to creating opportunities to go into men's rooms solely to wash his hands or comb his hair so that he could calm himself in the presence of other men at urinals.

1. Imagine yourself in a restroom situation that intimidates you. Go through the process (always in your mind) of walking into the room and finding a disconcerting situation. What will you do? Imagine yourself doing the next step successfully. For example, imagine a urinal right next to the sink without so much as a flimsy barrier/wall between you and the man washing his hands. You walk up to the urinal without hesitating. You unzip and take your penis out and hold it. You stand there comfortably. The urine does not have to flow immediately. The urine begins to travel down the urethra and soon it is flowing. Imagine you speak to the man once you've been successful at imagining urinating.

As you do this visualization, notice your feelings. Are you merely nervous, or are you tense? Or, are you filled with terror? (If so, your visualization was too far out and you need to imagine an easier challenge.) What thoughts did you have? Did you think something like, "What a looser I am?" or "This guy's intent on checking out my penis." What do your thoughts reveal to you about where you are coming from? (Below I have a section on affirmations which will help with thought management.)

Imagining a scenario similar to the one described on page 42, I might visualize the restroom and the man combing his hair and the urinals without partitions and with big basins of water. Having done that, I would now visualize going up to a urinal and successfully urinating.

2. Go to a restroom with a set up that is just beyond what you can pee in now. When someone walks in, visualize peeing next to him. You can listen to his urine. Imagine your own urine making the noise. What feelings and thoughts do you have? What do they say about you and your inhibition? Up the ante by imagining a conversation between you and another man in the restroom.

If you have reservations like "Right, no way I'll do that!" let go of your doubt. Keep reassuring yourself that, in this fantasy, you are capable of doing what you are imagining. You are progressing towards freedom.

Exercise

In your journal:

✔ Write your list of exposure rankings vis-a-vis the presence of other men. Realize that dealing with the occupants is a more complex situation than dealing with the rest room itself (it seems odd to make the distinction but doing so was useful to me).

✔ As with the restroom itself, write about your attempts at baseline situations for at least three or four times to ascertain that you are not fooling yourself about your level.

✔ Once you have been successful 3 or 4 times, move on to item number two on your list.

---

3. In either of the above scenarios, imagine:

A. you tell the man you have an inhibition around peeing in public and are working on a behavior modification program. Say it would be helpful if he witnessed you non-judgmentally. Experience the man being supportive. (Since this is your fantasy, you can make it go where you want. You are working with the parasympathetic system.) Rehearse the situations that intimidate the part of you that is stuck.

B. you are inhibited and waiting until he leaves.

Imagine it being all right to wait. You are all right even if you have to put off urinating. This is a good practice for seeing you comfortably through being blocked. Remind yourself that paruresis is only part of your life.

Story from the Field

While at a conference, I entered a men's room that I had not reconnoitered. Even so, I felt somewhat comfortable, encouraged by the successes I had already experienced. I presumed that I would be able to apply previous 'victories" to this situation.

A man was combing his hair in front of large mirror. No problem. Then I noticed the mirror offered the man a full view of the urinals. Not only that but the urinals were low oval bowls that would necessitate I piss into the water—catching the sound of every drip. There were no walls or partitions between them. All so open with a man at a mirror on the opposite wall!

In spite of my initial confidence, the situation quickly began to freak me out, and I went into a stall where I waited for the man to exit. Then, I came out and pissed in a urinal.

All day afterwards, I was depressed, deflated, disjointed and disconnected from the conference, wanting to go home. It made me feel that something was wrong with me, something deficient, missing.

It was only later that I was able to ease up on myself and acknowledge that the restroom set up was just too much for me at my stage of recovery. It was all right, I finally told myself, for me to piss in a stall or even to wait the guy out and then, as I did when I was alone, to practice the next step at the urinal.

C. you give yourself permission to go into a toilet stall when another man is present—or leave the restroom altogether. This reinforces your ability to choose. You always have the choice of a stall or leaving. You do not have to be emotionally violent to yourself. Knowing you have choices, you are minimizing occasions of failure. It is far better (in my opinion) to go into a stall to urinate than to stand at a urinal next to someone and be completely unable to let go. This can reinforce inhibition.

From now on, you can have comfortable and increasingly successful men's room experiences.

The choice is yours.

Finish Practice or Rehearsal on a Positive Note— Always

Finishing on a positive note is important. One study of people who had had a colonoscopy demonstrated this clearly. People who had had only the experience of the scope going in (a generally painful experience) and out (a less painful but still challenging experience) subsequently described the process as painful and were reluctant to submit themselves to it again. When doctors did the exact same procedure but allowed the scope to remain in the rectum for a few minutes (thus allowing for a neutral experience to terminate the colonoscopy), people described the entire process as less painful and were more willing to undergo another colonoscopy.

My conclusion for behavior modification is to finish every exposure experience—whether successful or not—on a positive note. This can be done in any of several ways.

✓ Celebrate your courage: "I would never have tried this a few months ago. I am so courageous now."

✓ Note how far you went: "I actually stood next to another man! It's only a matter of time before I can urinate easily next to another man!"

✓ Plan the next exposure: "Building on this time, I will repeat this exposure until I do it successfully."

✓ Honor your wisdom: "It was appropriate of me to leave. The situation was too much. It's wonderful how I can take better care of myself."

The idea is to experience the situation as another step towards success—not as a demonstration of your inability to change. Be creative in your responses and never label an experience as a failure.

Affirmations

Affirmations are positive statements we tell ourselves about future behaviors, events, and feelings. They are a step forward to changing how we think of ourselves.

Affirmations can be practiced anywhere and anytime, but especially effective are quiet times of which meditations—because they connect you with the parasympathetic nervous system—are prime examples. Once you have entered a quiet mode, repeat your affirmations. I have both memorized short lists and have read from a piece of paper for longer ones.

Affirmations must be positive; they often are stated in a progressive form (e.g., "more and more"); and they must be about you.

✓ "More and more, I am learning to urinate easily in a men's room with others present."

✓ "I honor my basic functions of urinating by responding to my body's needs."

✓ "Men's rooms are increasingly safe places for me to urinate."

✓ "Every day, I am becoming more open about peeing in front of others."

✓ "Every day, I connect to my fear and see it as empty."

When I enter a men's room, I still sometimes say affirmations like these to myself and visualize myself being successful. I also breathe deeply!

Warnings About Visualizations and Affirmations

If your practice of visualizations and affirmations seems counterproductive (you find yourself reinforcing doubt), look at your content and the wording. Do they contain a negative ("I don't get frozen") or are so far beyond your current stage that they defy credibility? ("I am urinating at a trough with newspaper reporters interviewing me for a paruresis article.")

Visualizations and affirmations are not substitutes for graduated exposure. They are preludes for men who wish to have an intermediate step between hoping and execution. They are tools—no more no less.

The ultimate tool is always graduated exposure.

Facing Your Fear of Being Blocked

This is something I have not done but I have read about it and am presenting it to you in the case that you might want to try it.

In a real way, what you and I are afraid of may

not be urinating in front of others. At least, many of us can continue a flow once it is started. That is, if I have begun to urinate before someone else walks into the rest room, I am generally able to empty my bladder.

What I used to find hard to do—and still sometimes do—is to **start** in the presence of others. My fear then seems to be I will be blocked in the presence of others if I try to start to urinate.

One suggested remedy for this is to confront your fear head on. You do this by going to a public urinal and standing there without any attempt to urinate. As men come and go next to you, you merely stand there and face your fear. You do not attempt to urinate. You let thoughts race through your mind, note them, and let them go.

In this way, your fear of being blocked is minimized. The idea seems to be that you have proven to yourself that you can stand there and not urinate. You have proven you can handle your fear.

Perhaps this will work for you. I have never tried it as it did not appeal to me. I did not want to re-traumatize myself, which I felt is what it would do, but I have read of others who have used this technique successfully.

Chapter 4: Pee Buddies

Shame-based behaviors thrive on silence. Your shame about not being able to urinate easily—or at all—in public leads you to isolate yourself. Somebody/something got to you once (most likely when you were little) and taught you that your body functions (and, by extension, you!) were wrong, or dirty, or defective.

The fact is your functions—and you!—are ok.

This inhibition about peeing in front of others is separate from you. You can let it go. This is what this book is about. It is about learning to let go of shame and accessing your birthright.

You need to go public about your inhibition—both in what you say and what you do. That doesn't mean you have to announce it (or do it) from the rooftops. Go public with your best man friend first. (The woman of your life is another person you need to "out" yourself with if you haven't already done so, but generally men do not relieve themselves in the presence of women so there is no need to "out" yourself to other female acquaintences.) Speak to your friend about being pee shy. Then ask him to witness you urinating.

"A good friend is cheaper than therapy."

"I can't possibly ask or do that!" you say.

Why not? Aren't friends supposed to support one another? Do you need to evaluate the quality of what you presumed to be a friendship?

Broaching the Subject with Your Best Friend

"How would I ever broach the subject?" you ask aghast. "Much less urinate in front of him!"

✓ You might say the following: "There's something I need to talk to you about. It's hard for me, but I need to ask you something." There might be a long silence. Commit yourself to not quitting. Decide that you will not leave until you have said what you need to say. (Be sure you don't approach your friend at a time when he will be rushed to move on and so provide you with an easy evasion of the task at hand!) This inhibition has you in its grip, not your friend. Your friend loves you: he will want to help.

In your request, tell your friend that all you need from him is for him to stand with you (in back of you, next to you, or in front of you—your choice) while you urinate. Your friend need do nothing but support you by witnessing you. (I followed this procedure many times.)

✓ If it's easier, write an e-mail or letter to your friend. (This is what I did with my best friend. It was my first request.) Go ahead, do it now! You can write in the calm of your home. You can write and rewrite the message until you feel you've gotten it right. Ask your friend for a response—either in person, by phone, or by e-mail/mail. Then send the e-mail or mail the letter immediately. Drive to the post office if necessary so that you don't allow yourself the opportunity to change your mind and trash the letter.

When a positive answer comes back, set up a practice time. Beforehand, let your urine fill your bladder. Drink extra water if necessary. Do not urinate for at least several hours before the attempt!

You will be nervous, but do not back down. Tell your friend you are nervous. It is best not to go to a public restroom since other men night be coming in and out and you shouldn't have to deal with them. (What you are doing will intimidate you enough without other men adding to the difficulty!) Even a public single-user toilet is not a good choice since you may be subjected to knocking on the door from an impatient person next in line, or you may be afraid someone is waiting outside and you will soon hear knocking on the door. Obviously, this would inhibit you. Use a home toilet—or, even better, the great outdoors. I recommend the outdoors because you will be so nervous that it will be useful not to have to worry about directing your urine into the bowl.

Two developments are likely. Your penis might shrivel up and you won't have much to hold on to. Conversely your penis might engorge, and you will find yourself embarrassed to be having a semi-erection and spraying messily.

Ask your friend beforehand to assure you, in so many words, that he will wait as long as it takes for you to urinate. Conversation can help—about your inhibition or about anything at all. Eventually even if it takes ten minutes or twenty, you will experience yourself relax and the urine will flow. (Remember all that water you drank earlier!)

Congratulations! You have taken another great step towards overcoming your paruresis. This may be the first time in your life that you have urinated so publicly—be assured that it will not be your last! Urinating in front of another man is a normal thing. Being uptight is what is not normal. You are moving towards normalcy.

Story from the Field
from a journal entry

After I arrived last night, before going to bed on the first night of my visit, Jeff asked me if I wanted to start the behavior modification experiment I had written to him about, and I said, "No, I am too tired. Tomorrow."

Today, I am resolved to go ahead. When I awoke and looked into his room, I saw that he was gone. I decided to foregone urinating alone and to wait for his return. I am nervous.

I feel infantilized by this hang up. I do not want it in my life. (I also do not want to go through with the behavior modification scheme I have devised. It is too weird!)

I held my night urine in, and my bladder was more than full by the time Jeff returned.

"If you're ready...?" I asked.

"Let's go for it," he assured me. "I have to go, too."

Jeff and I went outside to his lawn which is absolutely private, and we stood side by side. He peed quickly and easily. I stood with my penis in hand, completely blocked.

"This is scary stuff for me," I said, looking out on the lake.

I talked about what I was experiencing in my body. My voice was shaky. My legs were trembling. Because I was so nervous, my penis had shrunken. We both looked at my penis. It was so small! Then Jeff made some small talk about the clouds and the possibility of rain and how we needed rain.

After a long time, but not excruciating as Jeff was not judgmental of me—he just waited patiently for me to be ready, I felt a trickle coming. I mentioned it. He looked at my penis as a few drops came out and raised his eyebrows in sympathy. What a friend!

Nothing more was happening, but I had an odd sense that I would pee soon in spite of being blocked just then. Then I felt it coming. I began to urinate in a trickle. It took a long time, and for a while, it was just a dribble. Finally, I was done.

Jeff asked, "Is that what you wanted of me?"

It was. What I had wanted was a male witness. Finally, I had done it. I had urinated in front of another man.

I began to shake a lot, my whole body shook, my teeth chattered. Waves of anxiety and repressed feelings swept over me, but it felt good.

I am sitting alone on the dock as I write this. Have I really gone into a new stage even if I know it can only be called a beginning stage? I will succeed in this struggle to be free to urinate. I am committed while here to urinating as frequently as possible with Jeff as my witness.

*

My experiment with Jeff continues. Several hours later, we were at the boat launch working on his boat cradle. I had to go "wicked bad." I asked him to witness me again. We went a short way into the woods, and he urinated, too. (I am impressed with how easily he urinates—"like brushing my teeth," he says.)

My own urination came easily. Even though I had let my bladder get very full, I was surprised I urinated. None of the long wait of the morning.

Much later, as we were going back up to the boathouse, we urinated together again. I was surprised once more that it was not very hard.

Towards the end of the afternoon, Jeff said, "Well, I think it's about time to whip it out and have another session!" And I peed on his lawn with him. In the evening, we went out to eat, and, coming back, he stopped on the side of the road (after having taken a side road) and we both stood together next to his car. It was the first time while traveling that I had ever gotten out of a car and peed with another man, but it felt so normal. (How many times have I suffered with too much urine that I would not allow myself to discharge in front of another man traveler? How many times have I passed up an opportunity to relieve myself and have had to agonize the long miles still to traverse until I would have another opportunity to urinate?)

Later, we talked for a long time on his dock. I remember feeling my bladder filling—thinking "the problem is coming on!" Then, I realized that urinating was not a problem with Jeff. It was something I could do when I needed to do it. When we went up from the dock, I stood next to Jeff but, just then, to my surprise, I had a hard time (as in my first time in the morning). I did not panic but told Jeff I was blocked. That openness relaxed me a bit. I just stood there patiently and eventually the flow came.

Is there some part of this inhibition that is associated with nighttime? Is that why it was harder?

*

This morning, Jeff had already peed. When he told me in an almost apologetic way, I answered, "This experiment is about me not about you."

We went outside. I could not urinate. We went in to have breakfast and before he left to go do some tasks, he asked if I wanted to try again. I did and I was able to. The flow was a bit reluctant but it came. Why the variation in outcome?

I have been nervous all the while I have been doing this practice. How will I ever transfer it from something I do in the safety that Jeff creates to one that is less structured and more threatening?

When I go into a public restroom, I block up as I did this morning. If I can't pee right away, I am sure I am being judged and put down. I know that it is unlikely that anyone notices or cares, but, when I am in that restroom, I am blocked. It is as if thunder—attracting everyone's attention—were clasping around me. I shrivel up, "want to die," I feel like I am less of a man. I feel deficient.

*

I have to urinate again. I will have to do so in the next half hour. Since we are in town, it will probably be in an indoor toilet. Indoor toilets intimidate me—when someone is around. Public toilets are the scenes of my failures, the bane of my life. I'm both looking forward to trying out a men's room with Jeff and apprehensive. How will it challenge me? Will I completely block up? What if a third man enters or is there to begin with? (I always feel like hiding. It is my shame. I always feel like I will be found out and what I need to do is protect myself, take care of myself by running away.)

When I told Jeff, he said, "I need to take a leak, too. Let's go." We walked into the library, to the men's room. There was a stall and a urinal. I started for the urinal, but Jeff pointed to the stall, which was handicapped accessible, and said, "There'll be enough room in this stall for us both to piss together." His attention to my experiment rally touched me. We went in, one on each side of the toilet, and urinated, he coming faster than I, but that was ok. Being in a new environment, inside in a men's room, made me nervous. It was good to begin to explore that. Men's rooms have frequently been the source of great embarrassment. It was with great satisfaction therefore that I walked out of the bathroom with Jeff—feeling that I hade accomplished a very masculine thing. It was as if I were strutting in front of the world. "See

I'm a normal man who urinated in a men's room. See I'm walking out at the same time as another man."

After that, I urinated perhaps once before lunch, but, later after talking with the computer man Jeff had introduced me to, I came back and Jeff was up at the house. He didn't need to go so I peed alone with him next to me. That seems a real progress. Later urinations were not very special in difficulty or circumstance. The next day, my third and final day, waking up, I did not have any problem as I had had the previous day. Before leaving at 9:15, I went up to my car and Jeff was doing something around his car. I suggested we go one last time behind the garage. We did, and I beat him to it. That was the first time. He said, "You've done a lot of work these last few days."

Yes, I have. I am not sure how it can transfer, but I am determined to find out how and implement it.

More on Speaking to Other Men

To overcome your shame, commit yourself to urinating in front of male friends and acquaintances whenever appropriate—every occasion it is appropriate! The first time you ask anyone to witness you will be the most difficult time. Do so as soon as possible! Get it over with! Then keep asking.

Like all behaviors, urinating in front of others will become easier the more you do it. That's the strength of exposure work. Urinating with a man you have asked to witness you is both easier and more difficult than doing so with a stranger.

It is easier because you can select men who will not judge you and so you can eliminate—or at least mitigate—any consequent feeling of failure. If it takes you ten minutes or more to relax, that's fine. Your man will not shake his head or judge you or walk away.

It is harder because you're doing something without any "protection." No anonymity, no little wall between your penis and someone's stare. It's all out there. It's going "all the way," and other experiences of public urination may then seem less challenging or threatening—and that's what you want. This witnessing can also speed up the process. Many times when you walk into a men's room, however, you are alone in the space and therefore cannot practice acquiring new behaviors. That slows progress. Every time you ask someone to witness you, you will be asssured someone is there and you will be unlearning an old behavior and practicing a new one.

If you habitually pass up opportunities to urinate in the presence of others (male friends and acquaintances), ask yourself why you foregoing the chance to develop new behavior. Why are you holding on to shame? In answering this, don't be too easy on yourself. There are years of fear weighing against change. It is likely your answer will be a justification rather than a valid reason.

Behavior modification calls for tireless activity. Commit yourself to urinating—whenever appropriate— only in the presence of other men—strangers in a rest room or pee buddies. It's what you need to do if you are going to modify your behavior. Thinking about change in you behavior, hoping for change, will not effect change. Only making a modification in your behavior will create a change in your behavior. With every succeeding effort, the asking will be easier (and the doing, too).

Notes on Witnessing

Where are you comfortable having your witness stand? For some men, the witness must stand many feet away or one of you will have to be behind a bush or a door. For other men, the witness will be immediately behind them or next to them. I almost always asked the man to stand in front of me—I was so avid to beat this thing.

If the man who had agreed to witness me looked away, I asked him to look directly at me—or even at my penis. (Why not go for broke in attacking your inhibition? Looking away is in itself a shame-based behavior and you do not need someone else's shame.)

If you want your man to stand somewhat close and he stands at a distance, ask him to move closer—say within a few feet. (Obviously, to make these requests you've had to put some thought to selecting men who would be amenable to following your suggestions.)

Don't involve men who may make the experience about them. This is about you—at your stage of freeing yourself from paruresis.

As with rest rooms, you may set up a list of pee buddy challenges and work your way to your best case scenario.

Other Things to Consider

Eventually you may ask several men at a time to witness you. Does this produce an adrenaline rush in you right now as you read this? Know it will be possible for you to do this as you progress through this system. (Ultimately, isn't your goal to urinate easily and freely without inhibition and shame in any appropriate situation—even at the urinal trough with men at either side talking with you!)

Remember that every exposure ought to contain a positive effect. Even if you totally block up, you can congratulate yourself for having made the effort. ("Last month at this time, I would never even have tried this situation. My doing so is an indication that I am proceeding towards my goal.")

Even as I urge you to go public, I also offer you the counsel that it is all right to keep your privacy. You do not need to court more shame and disapproval. Choose your challenges prudently. But remember always that shame is isolating and that the way through shame is to become public, to break the silence. If you hold on too frequently and strenuously to being private, ask yourself what you are holding on to. Are you holding on to your shame? Do you really think holding on will free you?

What is certain is that, if you want to get rid of shame, you must destroy the privacy and silence that nurtures it. Once you do, you will be amazed at how doable what had seemed undo-able is.

Exercise

✓ Make a list of men you know and trust in front of whom it would be appropriate to urinate. (Do not choose men who will be uncomfortable or who will be worried about homophobia. Dealing with a man's fear of your penis is not what you need to do right now.)

✓ Ask each man on your list (in due time—but don't put it off) to witness you. Some of these men, you will discover, may be pee inhibited themselves. Welcome them to join you in the experiment. But don't push them. I am not proposing that you undertake changing their inhibitions. That is their choice not yours.

> ## Story from the Field
>
> Over the next 3 to 5 years after my experience with Jeff, I asked many men to witness me. Along the way, some men refused, but most said yes. Every once in a while, someone would quip, "This is a joke, right!?"
>
> Incredible as it may sound (and the number astounds me today!), at least 50 men agreed to help me. Asking became almost like a compulsion! I was so determined to succeed! (Many of the men I asked, I hardly knew.)
>
> I would request that the willing men stand in front of me as I felt that upped the ante. I felt too impatient for progress to fool around with men twenty feet in back of me and then ten feet, and so forth. (But, if that's what you need to do, that's all right!)
>
> With this much practice, I really loosened up.
>
> I look back on this experience as an incredible feat of which I am proud.

Success Enhancers

Identify elements in yourself that will lead to success. Each man with bashful bladder has a separate list of factors that make public urination easier or harder.

✓ **Fullness of bladder.** For many men, a bladder that is full to bursting will make it easier to urinate in front of others. During early phases of behavior modification, if your bladder is not full, it is prudent to hold off urination in front of others until it is.

✓ **Not every man needs to know about your bashful bladder.** There are likely men with whom you will never speak about this. They do not feel safe to you. (Why would you choose to confide in this man? Be sure the issue is about him and not about you.) Until you are far along with your behavior modification, avoid these men. Later, they may serve you in one of your graduated exposure steps—but not now.

✓ **Holding yourself emotionally separate.** Some men find it easier to urinate if they avoid eye contact or conversation with others in the room. They may repeat to themselves, "I really don't care what they think of me. They are not important to me. They are nobodies in my life." I do not believe this is a positive reaction as it feels to me to be shamed-based. For a while, however, you may find this negative response to others useful. Eventually you can work your way to being emotionally open as you enter a restroom.

Some men close themselves to a point of having hateful and condemnatory thoughts about other men to help them urinate. I don't think this is acceptable even for a short time. Why would you want to fill your mind with negative thoughts?

To some extent, your openness or closeness mirrors your openness and closeness with men in general. Accept it as an indicator of work needing to be done—or successfully achieved.

✓ **Appreciating that practice itself, especially in its early stages, can make you very nervous and tense.** This is the result of your old self-concept resisting new behaviors. ("I'm not a man who can...") As you explore new personal identities, you are bound to be uncomfortable.

In looking into your past and into you emotions, it's not that you should dwell there. You do, however, need to know what thoughts are crowding into your mind, often filling it with terror and fear.

In journaling about your current men's room

experiences, you will learn much about the feelings that dominate you in situations where others are present when you need to urinate. These feelings obviously lead to behaviors. If you can alter the feelings, you can alter the behaviors and vice versa.

The info-gathering journal exercise below must be repeated every little while to assess where you are currently at. You might say, "I already know that stuff," but journal writing has a way of creating additional clarity.

Exercise

In your journal, write of your present men's room experiences. This will help you appreciate the nature of your feelings. What feeling do you have:
- ✓ when you first realize you need to urinate?
- ✓ when you are outside the restroom door?
- ✓ when you first enter the room?
- ✓ when you see the room's disposition? (That's why you made an inventory of men's rooms in your area—to minimize the unknown)
- ✓ when you find out there is someone else there?
- ✓ when you select the urinal you will go to?
- ✓ when you approach the urinal?
- ✓ when you first reach for your penis?
- ✓ when you pull it out?
- ✓ when you stand at the urinal before peeing?
- ✓ when you realize that you might be blocked?
- ✓ when you stand there blocked?
- ✓ when you finally start to urinate?
- ✓ when you accept being blocked and walk away?

Chapter 5: Your Emotions

In this chapter, I will write about feelings you are likely to experience as you do exposure work and how you can use your observant self to analyze these emotions.

Anxiety and Fear

It's almost a given you will be anxious and fearful every step of the way as you modify your paruretic behavior. What you are doing—changing behaviors that may reach back to your boyhood, behaviors that you may have had for a lifetime—is very hard to effect.

"Always do what you are afraid to do."

—R. W. Emerson

Your paruresis arose to protect you from situations that were threatening—either really or seemingly. Now as you undo paruretic behavior, you may find yourself very fearful of "phantom" threats (i.e., threats from the past and not from the present.) For instance, sometimes you will enter a restroom and you will not understand why you feel overcome with negative feelings. You'll think, "This behavior modification is not working. Paruresis is too difficult to overcome."

"Why can't it all go away!" you may bemoan. The fact is, left to itself, peruresis is not likely to go away. On the contrary, it will probably get worse. Some men carry paruresis with them into their old age and die without ever mastering it. But, you do not want to settle for that.

I'm sorry that you are afflicted with paruresis, but you are and that's that. Now let's move on. Don't give in to your anxiety and fear. Instead, refer to your observant self. Say to yourself, "I am anxious and fearful about something in the past." Then say, "And I will use a urinal. It is safe to urinate today in the presence of other men."

Your observant self can look at your fear. What is it that is making you so uncomfortable? Are these issues you can work on in your journal? What affirmations can you create to counter your fears?

Give Yourself a Break

Sometimes, however, you can simply give yourself a break. It's all right to decide, "I'm taking it easy today." For one day, use a stall. But, "break taking" needs to be kept to a minimum. It is an exception to the behavior you have now committed yourself to—using public men's restrooms unself-consciously and/or urinating outside freely in the presence of others.

I was always looking outside myself for strength and confidence but it comes from within. It is there all the time.

—Anna Freud

Whom is all this hard work for? Well, it's for you! Who will give you kudos? Well, the man you will be one day who is paruresis free.

Emotional Work With the Past (More on Possible Origins of Your Paruresis)

Examining the past is important work, but it can be an energy sink. While it is an adjunct task and not a central one and while you can alter the hold of paruresis in your life without doing this introspection, examining the past can also be catalytic. Since shame-based behavior is learned from other people (wittingly or unwittingly) and from circumstance, it may be useful to your recovery to examine the origins of this shame (see page 15). This is done by looking into your past for triggers. Awareness of these triggers will inform you about how external to you your shame is. It is not you; it is something you do. That realization is perhaps the biggest benefit of looking into the past.

In the process of examining your past, there is some risk, varying according to your personality bent, that you will get caught in intellectualization and put off the essence of change: behavior modification. You can spend a great deal of time and energy thinking about behavior and completely fail to implement change strategies. Thinking about change is not the same as making change happen.

Reviewing specific areas of your past can be very revealing. These often have included an adult who was impatient or disapproving. In addition to the probable causes mentioned in Chapter One, look into:

✓ **toilet experiences in which you wet the floor or seat or wet your clothes.** Did you take too long from the point of view of an adult care provider? Were you ridiculed (being labeled "cute" can be a form of ridicule) by a male or female adult for the size of your penis?

✓ **nudity as an occasion of being shamed,** a huge taboo, or discomfort associated with body parts leading to an associated fear of sticking your penis out to urinate in the presence of others.

✓ **attitudes towards men in your family—** dirty, irresponsible, penis driven. Who wants to do a male-identified activity like pissing from an exposed penis?

✓ **incest or sexual exhibitionism directed towards you or some child near you.** This can include the emotional transference of your mother's affection and attention from your father to you, a too 'sticky" attachment.

As you do this introspection work, memories will inevitably surface and you may see how they are connected with your inhibition. The more you write, the more you will remember. Naming an experience can be a way of releasing its hold on you and turning things around.

Here are a few activities you can do with these memories:

✓ **forgive other people who were involved.** Do so in your head, via a role play or in writing that you do not send. Sending such writing can lead to renewed interaction that can be negative. Healing and not re-traumatization is what you are seeking now.

✓ **assure that part of yourself (that is "the child within") that these memories are from the past** and "the child within" is safe now with the adult you have become.

✓ **assert your right to move on with your life**

Exercise

In your journal, write about an early life experience that may be linked with urination—even remotely.

✓ Include as much detail as you can. Insert conversations and descriptions.

✓ If you are so inclined, rework this memory as a fiction story or poem. Label this writing as story or poem. Rewriting experiences as fiction can help you access viscereal memories. You may be surprised at how well it can work.

---

and to become pee free.

Cognitive Therapy

If you change how you express yourself, you can also change how you feel—to some extent. This is the basis of what is called cognitive therapy.

Exchange one set of negative fear-inducing words for other words that support you and your effort. For instance, stop thinking and saying 'problem." You can say "challenge" or "a decision to be made." Instead of saying "This is awful" you can say "This is not what I expected." "This is the worst thing ever—being in a rest room with other men and being blocked" can become "This situation can apprise me of where I am at in dealing with my paruresis and help me to write up a new exposure ranking list."

Cognitive reconditioning is not about lying to yourself or making a new reality up. It is about expressing the reality before you in a way that supports you rather than defeats you. Cognitive therapy, as the name suggests, is about altering the way you think about situations and people.

Emotional Work With the Present

Remember that you can choose to give yourself positive messages. That's what affirmations are about. They are not magic bullets but another tool to use to change your behavior. To learn to do so effectively will take a while—even perhaps a long while—but it can be done. Repeat your affirmations even if you don't believe them.

In the earlier section on affirmations, you created positive sentence to help you change. This section builds on that one. Take the information you have gleaned from monitoring your behavior and from the memories you have written about and create affirmations for yourself to counter your negative feeling from the past.

   ✓ "Urination is a normal function I engage in with increasing ease."

   ✓ "Men are beautiful and how they urinate is beautiful."

   ✓ "I am a healthy man, engaging in a healthy function."

   ✓ "The men's room is a safe environment, and there is no one there from my past to hurt me."

   ✓ "My body is fine with all its imperfections."

These affirmations counter negative signals it is likely you were given for a long time about private or public urination. When the outside stimulus stopped, you probably began to give them to yourself. It is even possible that you were given negative messages about something else and you have transferred those messages to urinating.

The source of your paruresis is perhaps not crucially important. What is very important is that you end the trash talk you speak to yourself and learn to be more kind to yourself. Do not let the past occupy the present.

An example of the power of affirmations occurred when I quit smoking many years ago. I hoped to support my goal to do so by changing the way I thought of myself. As we all have, I had been subjected to countless advertisements in which a smoker is portrayed as attractive, "cool," or special in some way that was associated with smoking. Knowing this to be the case, I knew I had to change the way I thought of myself if I were to quit smoking.

I kept affirming, "I am a person who does not smoke." (An unusual instance when an affirmation is stated in the negative.) I also said things to myself like, "I enjoy having healthy lungs," and "I enjoy smelling fresh and clean." I repeated this even when I was smoking and surrounded in a cloud of stench!

One day, perhaps a month after I had begun this behavior modification process, I felt very deeply that something had shifted. I said to myself, "What am I doing! I'm smoking and polluting my lungs! I am a person who does not smoke!" From then on, I was well on my way to becoming a person who does not smoke. (That was almost thirty-five years ago, and I have not smoked in all that while.)

After hearing yourself repeating an affirmation 100 times, 1,000 times, you will begin to believe its message. And that belief will be a tool to change your behavior.

If negative messages from the past could have changed your behavior for the worse, why can't positive, life-enhancing messages from the present change them for the better?

Chapter 6: Plateaus

Regular practice of behavior modification will definitely lead to progress. Some of the progress may be easy enough—becoming comfortable with scenes you visualize or affirm—and some remain, for awhile, decidedly beyond your capability—squeezing between two men at a long urinal trough. For now, however, you are noticing incremental, even if perhaps small, changes and for these you are grateful. Perhaps you have given yourself permission to use a stall and no longer ever have difficulty there. Perhaps you have spoken to a few friends and no longer have difficulty with them.

Then, one day, you notice that you have been at the same stage for a while. You are no longer making progress. You are at a standstill, stopped, idling on some plateau.

In my case, the plateau stage was frequently the result of slacking off with practice. It turned out that I was no longer attempting as many exposures as I had earlier. Perhaps I had not gone to a public restroom in a while. Perhaps I had grown comfortable with the guys with whom I could now urinate and I had forgotten to ask other, different men to help me. Perhaps I had not looked lately at my ranking of toilets arranged by degree of challenge and needed to up my difficulty of exposure.

Setbacks or Recidivism

The good news about a standstill is you are at least keeping your ground. In overcoming paruresis, however, there is a more disheartening stage: a setback or recidivism. At these moments, you may be discouraged that you have lost your hard-earned gains and are back to an earlier phase. What only recently had ceased to intimidate you is once again scary.

Unfortunately, this backward slide seems to be in the nature of a social phobia. Paruresis has been part of your life for so long that the imprint is rather fixed and deep and will reassert itself repeatedly.

"The key to change is to let go of fear."

Imagine you had mint or horseradish overtake your garden! You know how tenacious and invasive such plants can be. You also know that, if you persist in your attempts to eradicate these plants, you will succeed. Social phobias are like that, too.

In the end, no matter how tenacious paruresis is, if you consistently practice behavior modification you will succeed at eradicating it.

Exercise

Answer any or all of the following in your journal:

✔ Have you had setbacks recently? Describe.

✔ Were these setbacks repeated ones or just an occasional exception? Can you identify any causes?

✔ How did you react when you first noticed you were blocked? Did it feel like a debacle or a minor problem? (Hint: reframe debacles into minor problems.) Were you able to wrest some success out of this situation?

What to Do When You Have a Setback?

When you come to a setback—getting blocked in a restroom where you had urinated easily just a while earlier—or you go through a period of little progress, you may be tempted to wallow in negative feelings.

"I'll never lick this!"

"I was just kidding myself that I can be 'normal'."

"Why me?"

This is self-indulgent moaning. Don't give in to it. Instead let your observant self notice the negative feelings. Label what you identify ("Self-indulgent moaning is happening!").

After observing your reaction, move on. Ask yourself, "Where am I practicing today?"

Think of how inhibited you were before you began this behavior modification program. Recall the stories and strategies you had to concoct to have sufficient privacy to relieve yourself. Perhaps you could only go at home in the total privacy available there but now you can usually urinate in a toilet stall even if someone is in the room. It is not your goal, of course, to be contented with stalls, but being comfortable enough to use a stall in a public men's room is already a greater measure of freedom than you had before.

Perhaps you could pee in a public restroom but only if there were many urinals and you could distance yourself from other men but now you can pee in any size room providing there is a urinal between you and another man. That level, too, is not your ultimate goal, but it is already a greater freedom than you had before.

You continue to think: I was doing so well and now I keep having awful blockages.

Is all lost?

No! Why indulge in these thoughts?

✓ **Stay focused on your victories** even if a few have slipped away. If you could do the lost ones once, you can do them again.

✓ **Celebrate how some positive behaviors have almost become second nature now.** Perhaps you did block at a urinal recently but you can still go standing up in a stall. That used to be impossible—you used to sit down so as not to make noise. Celebrate your new baseline. Focus on that victory.

In the same way that you can eventually eradicate an invasive plant totally from a garden so, too, can you eradicate bashful bladder. One day, you will be completely uninhibited around the issue of pissing in front of other men.

Honor and celebrate whatever you have already achieved—and keep doing graduated exposure.

Possible Causes of Setbacks

I can come up with two plausible reasons for setbacks:

✓ **Advancing too fast beyond your level of achievement.** Perhaps you were doing fine in a row of three or four urinals with you at one end and some guy at the other. Then you walked into a two-urinal set up—the two were tight together. You went for it despite your misgivings—saddled up right next to the other guy. Freeze up time! Now, you have "awful-ized" this failure as "I'll never be able to be free of paruresis. That double urinal debacle proves it."

But, a setback is not permanent or universal. How many times has it occurred in your whole life? Once or twice? It is not the way things need to be—certainly not forever!

Don't get hung up on the too-difficult situation. First congratulate yourself for how far you have already come. A while back, you would never even have tried the double urinal! You're doing good work! (Remember the data on folks who had a mildly positive end experience with their colonoscopies? Spin a positive end to every exposure.)

Review your list of exposure rankings and ease yourself into a level of difficulty that is more appropriate for your stage of growth—even if that is now an item or two lower on your difficulty list. An appropriate situation is one you can deal with three or four times successfully. Then work your way up the list once again.

For example, as your next step in dealing with the two urinals cheek by jowl next to each other, you might choose to go to the urinals when the room is empty and to practice visualizing a man next to you—even visualizing speaking with the man. You might also practice in a room with three urinals if you are comfortable with that. Imagine the man at the third urinal is next to you. You might also look for a practice room with two urinals separated by a wall divider.

Keep reminding yourself that your setback is temporary and is due to factors you can alter, that some situations are clearly more difficult than others.

At first, especially if they are rushed into, difficult exposures may seem to offer only the possibility of failure. You do not need to pit yourself against this situation just yet. In fact, it's better not to try it. That said, push yourself, place yourself at the edge of your comfort and ability. It is the only way to change, to modify unacceptable social behavior.

✓ **Not practicing enough, repeatedly passing up behavior-modification opportunities.**

If effect, when this happens, you are "off the wagon." You are letting the mint and horseradish grow vigorously wherever they will in your garden rather than hoeing them down regularly!

Conversely, be patient with yourself. We all grow in spurts and starts, not in a regular pace. After you have been doing behavior modification a while, there may be times when all your effort will seem useless. When that happens, take note of how many new behaviors you have already been able to implement. It may truly astonish you to assess how much you have changed! Appreciate the great gap between urinating while sitting down in a stall and while standing in one. There is an equally large gap between urinating standing in a stall and doing so while standing at a long row of urinals with wall dividers. Acknowledge the changes and celebrate them.

It's also likely that you have been internalizing the change you have been implementing and are in fact making great strides in changing the way you think/feel about yourself with paruresis. Once your thinking catches up with where you're at, progress can begin again. Meanwhile, keep practicing.

Story from the field

A few years ago, I began working for myself in a home office and, as a result, began living a more isolated life. I did not have many easy opportunities to urinate where other men were present. Additionally, the friends I used to practice with had either moved away or I had lost the close connection I had with them. As a result of these two factors, I experienced a reversal in my freedom to urinate.

On the occasions when I did go to a public venue and approached a rest room, I found myself again playing the game of guessing if it was empty or not. Sometimes I stopped at a water fountain to allow time for anyone "lurking" in the men's room to come out. This was not a steady behavior however. There were still many times when I could walk into a rest room and urinate with someone there, but I could not do the trough as I once did.

This recidivism occurred so gradually and insidiously that I hardly noticed it until it was re-established and I was caught up in paruresis again.

I had almost licked paruresis about 12 years ago after giving it my hugely best shot. I was able to go with strangers almost anywhere under most conditions. I was at 8.5 on a scale of 10. (I was less successful with acquaintances.) Then gradually, I backslid to probably 4 or 5 (I need to celebrate that I had started at .5 and have never gone back there). There were still many successes, but never the full freedom.

In weightlifting, there is a term called "muscle memory." That means, if you have trained but have fallen off training, when you pickup again, your muscles "remember" and make quick progress once you resume.

I recommitted myself and have regained much. I intend to never backslide again. I'm not sure how, but I want this to be over—for good. The concept of muscle memory is one I am holding on to as I remember the recidivism of the past and hold onto the progress I have made. I want to obviate backsliding in the future.

Exercise

In your journal, answer the following:

✓ when you have a setback, how do you react? Is that reaction helpful to your success at behavior modification or will it likely lead to failure over the long run? At what point do you notice your reaction? At what point do you accept or refuse to change your reaction?

✓ to what was the setback due? Important here is to identify which of the circumstances you are capable of controlling and which you are not. That another man walked in right after you is beyond your control, but that you did not choose to go into a stall when you could feel blocking due to surpassing your exposure ranking is your decision. Going into a stall can put you back into a power position.

✓ Were they really setbacks or were you simply stopping work and reaping the results? This rest period can happen after a period of intense effort.

Chapter 7: BB Journal Entries

These are journal entries about men's experiences with behavior modification around bashful bladder.

Success with Exposure Work

My exposure work has been going fairly well. I have been going to a public rest room every day looking for exposure. Yesterday, I had a wonderful, encouraging experience. I was in a restaurant with two friends and went to the men's room when I felt the urge. (That's a great thing I am doing: going when I first feel the urge so as not to let tension build up.)

As I approached the door, another man went in ahead of me. I had never been in that rest room so I did not know what to expect. I figured that if there were two urinals one next to the other (beyond my exposure work now) that I would go into the stall. Inside the room there was a man at the sink which was separated from the urinal by a panel that was not a wall but went from the knees to the shoulders. The man who walked in ahead of me was in the one stall—standing up.

I felt an impulse to tense up and run but I said to myself, "No, that's not ok." I went to the urinal and unzipped and stood there with my penis in hand. "Oh my god! What am I doing? I'm going to freeze." But, I continued to breathe deeply and I said to myself, "That's not the story I want to tell about myself now. I just want to urinate and rejoin my friends. I'm tired of this drama." For a moment, I stood there, not urinating and then I reminded myself gently that urinating is not like turning a spigot on but that the urine comes from deep within my body and it is natural for it to take a moment to travel outward. I relaxed and, to my great amazement and joy, I could feel the urine descending—but would it stop?

The man was still at the sink about two feet away when my pee began to splash into the water of the urinal. I felt such release of energy. It was so wonderful to have a normal experience! Then I heard the man in the stall begin to pee. I realized that he must have some degree of paruresis. When I walked out of the restroom, I was feeling so good! Even today as I write about the experience, it feels like a breakthrough. For a moment, I was able to step out of the drama of "I can't piss in front of others."

I still can't believe that I pulled off that toilet experience last night.

Practicing a Slow Start

I have been practicing at home just starting off with holding my penis without urinating right away. Making "slow" a normal experience so that I can be comfortable at a urinal waiting for the urine to flow not right away but after a few moments.

Men's Room Lists

I realized that I was doing hit or miss sort of exposure. That is, I was not following the hierarchy I had made from easy to difficult. Sometimes I was even over challenging myself and so I was often unsuccessful.

I had made my list of do-able-to-impossible situations. I went back to it. I saw how I never have a misfire in a room with single toilet and never in a stall even if others are present. These do not challenge me and so they were crossed off my list

I can almost always do it in a single urinal if there is a wall rather than a separator. So the walled off urinal is my baseline because I am a bit nervous there only sometimes—really not often. So...

I have made a list of local urinals that are blocked off by a wall and I have decided to go to the next level of difficulty: talk to someone in the room. I did that yesterday and had a perfectly banal conversation about the great weather we were having and managed to pee. Today, in another rest room, I intended to have the conversation but just kept silent. Couldn't make myself talk but peed easily nonetheless. I have also decided to urinate into the water so that it is very clear to anyone what I am doing. I plan to have conversations in two situations before I move on to a harder exposure.

That harder exposure will be at a urinal that has only a divider or separator so that the other person can see my face and I can see his. I need to find several of these urinals locally.

A Technique that is Different

What worked for me was no longer using any muscular clenching to eliminate the final drops of urine at the end of urination.

I continue to practice this as it seemed very tangible, do-able. I'm not sure yet if it is helping me address being pee shy directly but it has given me several insights. John's suggestion of waiting for the final drops to flow has helped me realize a certain impatience to get the pee experience over with. [I've been telling myself that difficulty is no longer the storyline I wish to tell myself about my pee experience.] So... this practice has helped me to stay with the urination that is happening in the moment. Perhaps this will make it easier later to stand at a urinal? My experience of Friday evening [see above] can possibly be explained this way.

Another insight has been how much physical tension I feel surrounding the urination. This practice of not using muscular clenching has helped me to feel the tension and let go of it.

Fear of Not Urinating

It occurred to me recently that my fear is not of urinating in front of other men. It really is about NOT urinating. I am afraid of not being able to pee when I'm clearly trying to. Once I get going, I'm all set. So...isn't the phobia there in the beginning of the flow rather than during the voiding?

Chapter 8: FAQs

Q. Do women have bashful bladder?

A. Yes. In fact there is a book in the bibliography aimed at women paruretics (Olmert). Since paruresis is keyed to public urination and since public urination is often keyed to gender-specific toilets, I have chosen to write only about men in these pages.

"The only dumb question is the one you don't ask."

As a man, I only know men's rooms. Men's rooms call for much more public urination than women's rooms where every toilet is a stall, separated from one another by a wall. Men are constantly exposed to urinating openly in front of each other—often at urinals that offer no barrier from the sight of other men. As a rule, the male bashful bladder, I would guess, poses many more challenges therefore than the female variety.

This book does not deal with women and their bashful bladders because none of the "field work" was conducted with women.

That said, women could successfully adapt many of the strategies outline in these pages.

Q. Is it appropriate to aim toward urinating in front of women?

A. All our behaviors are to be judged for appropriateness. In North America, public restrooms are gender specific so that urinating before women is not an issue there. Elsewhere however, say while hiking of while playing sports, the issue might arise. Since we are people with shamed-based behaviors, we are prone to making compensatory errors in judgment to overcome our shame. Urinating in front of your female lifemate is certainly appropriate. In front of other women, however, I would take my cue from other men. And from the women themselves. I feel perfectly comfortable not having as a goal urinating in front of women. I feel hopeful that, if I were in a situation where I had to go, my ability to call on the relaxation factor would see me through.

Q. What if others think I'm odd or perverted as I exercise behavior modification practices?

A. What others think is their responsibility. What you choose to think is yours. The distinction is important.

That said, be appropriate, and behave within the norms of adult behavior.

Mostly, I would guess, however, that your concerns are about what people who are themselves damaged might think when they see you hesitate or take a long time to urinate. Do not worry about what they think.

Q. Can't I just live with this?

A. You have probably minimized your bashful bladder problem to confidantes. You have probably said, "I sometimes tighten up when I urinate in men's rooms" or "The flow of urine is not always full."

This is a function of your shame. The fact is you have suffered from the shame you carry with you. It has limited enjoyment of your life. What others do without a second thought has consumed your energy.

Why would you want to live with that for a second longer than you have to?

Q. If I practice behavior modification through gradual exposure in public venues, aren't I setting myself up for being judged harshly by other men?

A. The men in the restroom with you are just men like you. They urinate as one of the end products of eating and drinking. They are there to perform a bodily function—a completely natural one. You and they have the same urinary system that has to be daily attended to.

They are not there to judge you. In fact, they may not even be aware of you. Do not concentrate on their presence as they are not concentrating on you. If you find yourself concentrating on them, refocus your attention on urinating or on something else. (See meditation, page 26)

Much of toilet inhibition comes from fear of other men, of exposing one's self to others. Our penises are one of our most visibly male attributes.

Q. Is pee shy behavior different for circumcised men and uncircumcized men?

A. I don't know the answer to that one, but men who are circumcised produce a more focused and therefore more forceful stream of urine. An uncircumcised man in a public restroom may feel inhibited when he compares his own more dribbling flow to that of the circumcised man near him. This might be a case of confusing urination with ejaculation.

Q. I read someplace that you should get a medical exam to rule out that your paruresis is not physical in origin. What do you think?

A. I've read that, too, and it always seems to me like hedging bets. The fact is any man who is not an idiot knows whether his problem is mental or physical.

I never had any difficulty going at home or in a bathroom that is private so I knew for sure that this is not a physical problem. It's psychological all the way. Otherwise, I would have had problems at home or in a one-person room. I never did.

Q. What do you think of using a catheter?

A. I've never used one and I never would have, but then I have never had as severe a problem as some men do. It would have felt like a sure defeat for me. Perhaps useful for some men in a short-term impossible-to-go situation such as a transcontinental flight.

Q. Is male avoidant paruresis associated with effeminacy?

A. I have never made any connection between the two. I have seen effeminate men having trouble and macho men having trouble also. Nor do I think the problem is associated with one's sexual orientation. Or, at least there has never been a connection made in any of the chatrooms I have been in.

Chapter 9: Finishing

Will you ever be done with the bashful bladder?

The unfortunate—and truthful—answer is you will perhaps never be done with it. Like an alcoholic, you may always be at risk of slipping back into your old patterns.

In the same way that you should continue to take medication after physical symptoms have disappeared, so too should you continue to do your behavior modification program after you have achieved your goals and the symptoms of the shy bladder have disappeared. Recidivism is always possible. You spent years with inhibited behaviors and it is deeply ingrained within you and can resurface all too easily. Don't let that happen.

Continue to place yourself in difficult situations to assess your status. If you have slipped, resume your exposure work. If you are still fine, consider that the assessment has reinforced your new freedom.

What can unfortunately happen is that you say, "Oh,.I can urinate easily now in front of these men so I don't have to ask them to witness me." It's a bit like the alcoholic saying, "I don't need to worry about taking alcohol any more."

For a long time now, you have suffered from a shame-based behavior addiction and your deeply-ingrained tendency is to slink off to be by yourself. Keep at your exposure work even if you think you have overcome shy bladder. What often happens is you let off and, a month or two later, you find yourself right back in the throes of being uptight—almost as if you had never done any work at all. Keep scrutinizing your habits every day and asking yourself if you have been visualizing, affirming, role playing, having a man watch you (whenever appropriate), using challenging public restrooms, talking to people about it.

Don't think of this need to continue to do the work as oppressive. Think of it as your investment in your freedom and life.

How do you define success?

I suppose that depends on what you want to end with—not what you are willing to put up with.

Once I went into a restroom where there was a man doing cleaning and only the diabolic trough! Sure I could do it, I thought as I walked up to the trough. As I unzipped, I felt I was doing well so, to up the challenge, I started a conversation with the man. The flow came, and we talked the whole while I was urinating.

Me at a trough! A man swabbing the floor in back of me! Us talking! Incredible! It was something I had thought I would never see myself doing in my life.

I even developed the ability to go all the time with a number of my friends with whom I had spoken about paruresis. On nature walks, we would just go next to each other in the woods. Sometimes we would walk into a small restroom set up for only one person and urinate into the one toilet bowl. I loved it! I felt like a normal man. Hooray, it's over I thought. I'm normal!

But, inevitably there is always a risk of some recidivism. The trough experience is one I have not been able to repeat. Going next to a friend on a hike remains something I can do fairly easily.

Recently, I was at a friend's house. I had not spoken to him about paruresis. I had just entered his small apartment and, as he got me something to drink, I went to his bathroom which was just off the room in which we had been speaking. That room served as kitchen and livingroom. In the bathroom, I did not close the door, determined to push for an edge. There was a moment when I hesitated and I thought I'll embarrass myself big time. But no, I relaxed and let the urine descend—even if slowly. He chatted with me as I urinated. Incredible! I felt so normal!

So, success comes and goes, is sometimes elusive and, at other times, right there.

In all, most occasions are simply a lot easier, but none are really a given success. Even in a large room with movement—a setting that is almost never difficult for me now—I'll still be aware of paruresis. Unless I'm alone at home, I am never unaware of the possibility of freezing up.

But, life has gotten so much better. And...

If you do the work outlined in this book, you will know much success, too.

Bibliography

Agras, Stewart, M.D. *Panic/Facing Fears, Phobias, and Anxiety.* W.H. Freeman and Company, NY, 1985. An easy to read overview of fear, phobias and anxiety. Does not address paruresi.

McCullough, Christopher, Ph.D. *Free To Pee/ A Self-Help Guide for Men with Paruresis.* International Paruresis Association, n.d. A useful guide to overcoming paruresis. Helps make the process very do-able.

Olmert, Carol. *Bathrooms Make Me Nervous / a Guidebook for Women with Urination Anxiety (Shy Bladder).* 2008 Change strategies specifically for women.

Made in the USA
San Bernardino, CA
18 June 2016